Friendships 101

Identity, Confidence & Connections

5 WEEK SERIES

A HOW-TO CURRICULUM ON TEACHING GIRLS ABOUT BUILDING GOOD FRIENDSHIPS

Cover designed by Michaela Stromer

Interior designed by Jazlin Asencio, jazlinasencio@gmail.com

www.girls101.org   holly@girls101.org

Printed in the United States of America.

ISBN: 979-8-9871147-6-6

Acknowledgments

I want to thank my irreplaceable husband, and our amazing, God-given three daughters, who I love more than anything. Thank you to all the girls who have attended meetings through the years and made so many fun memories! Special thanks to the women who have been with me from the start, and many who have joined along the way. Thank you to Jazlin for helping me put this book together. And lastly, thank you to my best friend, Jesus, who somehow entrusted this fun adventure to me.

Table of Contents

Interact with us online!

We would love it if you post pictures on our social media pages so we can see your group:

www.facebook.com/Girls101Community

Instagram #girls101community

Welcome

We are elated that you want to lead a Girls 101 group.

Our Purpose

We provide a safe, fun atmosphere for girls to talk through life issues.

Our History

Girls 101 started as an after-school club in 2004. As a mom of three girls, I wanted to raise my girls to think critically, have high standards, be kind, and be able to see through the superficiality of the standards society set for girls. I also wanted them to have friends with a similar bent. I questioned the negative assumptions of society that girls would most likely become shallow, insecure, and mean to each other during their tween and teen years. I didn't believe it had to be that way.

Why were girls expected to fight with each other? Why did many girls become superficial and insecure during middle school? Why was it expected that moms and daughters would have a hard time getting along during teenage years? This didn't seem right to me, so we set out on a wing and a prayer in a long experiment to prove otherwise. Many moms, volunteers, school staff, and teachers gave of their time to help us get started. They believed in the cause. I'm very grateful.

Our original goal was to provide a community of mentors throughout the teenage years. As tweens and teens grow up, the need for a mentor is real, whether that mentor is a mom or another girl or woman a few steps ahead of her. Our goal was to help moms and girls stay connected during this time, allow moms to share parenting issues, and let our daughters see even more great examples of women around them. We wanted our girls to learn to think through issues for themselves while surrounded with friends and mentors who cared about them.

This curriculum is just one portion of what worked for us over the years. Feel free to adjust this to your group as needed. Whether your group is led by a teacher, a mom, a grandma, a mentor, or a young collegiate woman, this time spent with girls will be valuable to you and to them.

Girls LOVE to get together, talk, and discuss these topics that often go unaddressed.
This particular series is geared toward 4th-6th graders, but the joy is it can easily be adapted to younger or older girls. Over the last few years, we have found that five weeks is the perfect number of sessions per semester. It leaves the girls begging for more, is long enough for great lessons and bonding, and also allows your volunteers a break.

There are more series to come in this curriculum, but this will give you a great start! Enjoy!

Holly Tumpkin, Founder
holly@girls101.org

Introduction
Purpose

Girls 101 provides a safe, fun atmosphere for girls to talk through life issues—including identity and character, manners and body image, goals and choices, choosing good friendships and healthy relationships, and more.

Girls need a safe place to be with other girls and women who care about them, where they can discuss, process, and understand life together. When set in an environment of all girls, they are free to explore topics and interact freely without distraction.

We talk. We listen. We interact. We talk about subjects not always talked about. We hear issues of the heart.

Together, we explore and practice empowering solutions and skills for life. Along the way, friendships are made and fun is had. We've never had a group of girls who wanted the session to end. School atmospheres benefit, barriers are broken, and friends are made.

Mainstream culture highlights girls' insecurities, distorts their giftings, and does little to encourage them in setting meaningful life goals. To combat this, we focus on teaching girls what it takes to live well, make healthy choices, and lead purposeful lives.

Girls are girls wherever we go. Whether public, private, or homeschooled, privileged or not as privileged, they struggle with many of the same issues. We understand how great and specific the needs of girls are. Though girls may have different circumstances, they all share common bonds that can be defined, encouraged, and strengthened.

Girls 101 Outcomes

- What if girls in your school felt equipped to establish supportive relationships with other girls?

- What if they could learn and hone skills that will make them more confident in themselves and among their peers?

- What if, instead of creating drama, girls learned to get along?

Upon completion of this series, girls will be able to:

- Introduce herself to others
- Respectfully listen to others and get to know them
- Consider different places friends can be made
- Learn what qualities make a good friend
- Roleplay how to deal with friendship struggles
- Use the power of words intentionally

Leadership Expectations

- Facilitate a 90-minute meeting for five consecutive weeks.
- Recruit at least one volunteer to help run meetings, and be in touch with them weekly for reminders, support, and concerns.
- Gather small items for weekly prizes. (Your local dollar store is a great resource for these.)
- Be prepared each week with the lesson plan and all supplies needed.
- Have parents sign permission slips before posting any pictures of girls on social media.
- It's nice to take pictures during your meetings. A fun idea is to send a picture collage as a take-home gift at the end of your 5 weeks. Make sure you have parental consent before pictures are posted on social media.
- When girls arrive to the meeting, cell phones are put away until the meeting is dismissed.
- When real friendship issues are being discussed within the group, our rule is not to use real names of the friend. It is not an opportunity to gossip.

If meeting at a school, leaders also commit to:

- Abide by the school system's rules for checking in weekly as a volunteer, having parental permission before posting any pictures of girls on social media, and dismissing girls from each meeting to their appropriate way home.
- Sign up sheets are on page 78 for the school to use for getting parental permission to be a part of the group.
- In the rare circumstance that any unlawful subject comes up, you will make the school counselor or parents aware of the situation. Whatever is said in Girls 101 is confidential unless it is required to be reported by law.

Week-by-Week Outline

Week 1: Discussion on Girls and Friendships, Craft

- Purpose: Gain new friends, get to know old ones better, and become more knowledgeable of what makes friendships work.
- Discussion: Brainstorm about girls and friendships among girls. Do we label others without realizing it?
- Craft: Each girl will make a craft that represents herself to share with the group in Week 2.

Week 2: Introductions, Respect, and Listening Skills

- Purpose: Each girl will tell the group about herself. Girls will listen respectfully and ask useful questions to get to know each other better.
- Discussion: How to speak to a group, have respect, show good listening skills, and ask good questions. Sharing.
- Craft: Finish and share.

Week 3: Qualities that Make Good Friendships, Real Fights

- Purpose: Discover there are many places to find friends. Discuss qualities that build good friendships and qualities that cause conflicts among friends.
- Discussion: Talk about different types of friends and the advantages and disadvantages of having one best friend or numerous friends.
- Object lesson: Friendship Pie, Silhouette Friend, Snowball.

Week 4: Common Friendship Problems, Roleplay

- Purpose: Talk about common friendship conflicts that occur among girls and ways to handle them.
- Discussion: How girls and boys fight differently.
- Object lesson: Roleplay common friendship issues.

Week 5: Power of Words Craft, Hurtful & Helpful Words, Atmosphere Changers

- Purpose: Learn how words can be atmosphere changers.
- Discussion: How to throw away bad word memories, the strength of good word memories, your words can be atmosphere changers, making friends or losing friends by word choices.
- Craft: Word Box.

Games and Icebreakers

When you finish a lesson sooner than planned, or need a game to start a session, these are fun ideas:

- "I See" photography cards (available to purchase on www.girls101.org)
- "I Feel" quote cards (available to purchase on www.girls101.org)
- Girl Talk Jenga is a favorite of all ages (usually available in game stores or on Amazon).

Available to purchase on www.girls101.org

"I See" photography cards and *"I Feel"* quote cards are both valuable group facilitation tools. They are an evocative collection of photographs and quotes you can lay out for the girls to select one that represents how she feels in the present moment. It's an easy, fun, non-threatening way for girls to express themselves and leaders to get a sense for how individuals are feeling.

Old Favorites

The Telephone Game https://icebreakerideas.com/telephone-game (Girls still love to play this game!)

Blindfold Drawing. Have each girl close h er eyes while holding a pencil and paper. She must keeper eyes closed as you describe a scene to draw. (For instance, a tree on a mountain surrounded by flowers and a full sun.) When you say "Stop," let the girls show each other what they drew. If you have blindfolds for each girl, use them to cover their eyes. (Another way to play this is to have the girls put a piece of paper on top of their head and draw whatever you describe).

Don't Smile. Sit in a circle. One person tries to make someone laugh or smile. They can make faces or act silly or laugh, they just can't touch anyone. Whoever laughs or smiles is next.

Some are quiet,
Some are loud,
Some like karate,
Some like ballet.

Objective

In this lesson, we get to know each other and gain new friends. We consider taking off labels and open ourselves up to new ideas, new friends, and new possibilities.

Preparation and Materials

- Sign-in attendance sheet (Appendix page 77), pens.

- Copies of game (Appendix page 40), pens.

- Prize drawing: slips of paper should be available for each girl to write her name on one time.

- Prize bag full of prizes (Ideas- items from a dollar store,such as candy, notepads, socks, hairclips, stickers).

- A big note pad (at least 16x24) and markers should be at the front of the room, along with the rest of the items needed for today's lesson: sticky notes with pre-written thoughts, one blank poster (11x14) for each girl, poster decorations (markers, stickers, magazines, etc.).

- Make sure you have an ADULT VOLUNTEER selected to be "Sheila," and thoughts pre-written on enough sticky notes for each girl to have two.

- Make a poster about yourself ahead of time to show as an example (name, hobbies, favorite things, etc.).

- Have a camera or iPhone ready each week to take pictures.

Lesson at a Glance

Activity	What To Do	Materials
1. Welcome	Introduce Leaders	None
2. Girls 101 Expectations	Discuss boundaries for the group	None
3. Prize Bag	Pick names	Names in drawing bag, prizes
4. Get To Know You Game	Have one copy per girl	Appendix, Page 40
5. Discussion	Brainstorm about girls	Easel pad, markers
6. Labeling	Sticky thoughts	Pre-written thoughts on sticky notes
7. What Makes You You	Make a poster	11x14 posters, craft supplies (see page 15)
8. Group Picture	Take a picture	Camera/phone

Week 1 Lesson

Arrival (10 minutes) As girls arrive, sign in on attendance sheet, sign up for prize drawing, and put personal items aside.

Prize Bag

As each girl arrives, add their name to the drawing bag to win prizes. Each week names will be drawn to pick a prize. Everyone wins once. Everyone will win by the end of the series.

Greeting: *Welcome, everyone, to Girls 101.*
We're here to get to know new friends, play games, make crafts, and learn about life and friendships. We leaders love to spend time with you girls. We are honored to be here with you.

Girls 101 Expectations (5 minutes)

Explain the importance of keeping an open mind to making new friends and getting to know girls better.

There are a couple of things we want you to "take off" and "put on" when you come through the door every week.

- Take off negative thoughts at the door, like "I had a bad day", or "I'm mad at my friend. I don't want to be here today."
- Fights or conflict with anyone.
- Any vocal bad feelings towards each other are not welcomed in this group.

This is a place where everyone is welcome. Things to "put on" each week:

- The chance to make a new friend.
- Treat everyone in the group with respect.
- You don't have to like everyone, but no one should know who those people are that you don't care for.

In summary, when you walk in each week, take off bad thoughts and put on respect and openness towards each other.
(Have a girl volunteer to act out the "taking off" and "putting on" behaviors stated above—girls love to do this)

This program has happened at many other schools for the past several years. What has happened in the past is that girls got to know each other better and made more friends! That's what we want for you.

(Important note to leader: If you hear any mean words or fights going on during group time, the girls involved need to be warned once. If it happens again, they should be asked to go back to the school staff member for the day. If it happens consistently, some-one else will get that girl's slot, because there only a certain amount of spaces. If you are meeting in homes, have a volunteer pull the girl aside and talk to her about spoken words.)

Prize Bag

First thing each week, we'll draw for the winner of this week's prize. If your name is drawn, choose an item out of our prize bag to take home. Don't show others what is in the bag, so it will be a surprise when their turn comes. You have one minute to choose a prize. (Throw away the winners name, so they aren't chosen again. Each person wins one time.)

Get to Know You Game (10 minutes)

"Get to Know You" game in the Appendix page 40.

Discussion (7 minutes)

Now we're going to brainstorm about girls together: what are girls like? How do we differ from boys?

Tip: To help girls brainstorm, have a volunteer write out their responses on a big notepad that all can see.

Lead a discussion by asking the following questions. Any answers are ok! This is a brainstorming activity.

- What words come to mind when you think of girls?
- What are girls like?
- What are they good at?
- What do they do?
- What about girls and friendships?
- What are good things about friendships?
- What are bad or hard things about friendships?
- Are there a lot of cliques with girls at your school or not?
- Are girls easy or hard to get to know?

"Labeling" Activity (15 minutes)

For this activity, you will have PRE-MADE a stack of sticky notes with phrases written on them. Use oversized sticky notes. On each sticky note, pre-write a variety of thoughts like the ones listed—enough so each girl can read at least two.

Examples of pre-written phrases:

1. She's too pretty.
2. She's not pretty.
3. I heard about her; she got in trouble at her last school.
4. She looks too rich.
5. She looks too poor.
6. She seems too loud.
7. She seems too quiet.
8. Everyone may like her; she might steal my friends away; I better be mean to her.
9. Everyone may like her; she may try to take my place; I better act like I'm friends with her to watch her.
10. She looks nice; I bet we will be friends.
11. I bet she is scared; I better see if she wants to sit by me at lunch.
12. I saw the way he looked at her; I don't like her already.
13. She looks snotty/stuck up.
14. I already have enough friends.
15. I'm glad I'm not the new person!
16. I wonder if she'll be popular.
17. I saw the way she looked at me.

To start, use a volunteer or leader to stand in front of the group and be labeled during this activity. (Do not use a girl from the group.) The stand-up will be a "new girl at school." Her name is Sheila, and today is her first day of class. You are all sitting in class when Sheila walks in; she is new and no one has met her. (Sheila stands at front). As she walks in, we are all thinking different thoughts about her, though not saying them out loud. We all think things we don't say out loud.

Questions:
- Do we know anything at all about Sheila? (NO)
- Do we know yet if she's a good friend or bad friend? (NO)

One at a time, have each girl come up and read one of the large sticky notes you will give them. Then have the girl read the thought out loud before they stick the sticky note on Sheila. They can stick the sticky note anywhere on her—arms, legs, face, etc.

Once Sheila is all covered with thoughts and labels, discuss this visual representation of what our thoughts can do to people before we even know them. Talk about not knowing anything about her, and not even being able to see who she really is, especially now that she is covered with all of the assumptions we made about her without even knowing what kind of person she is.

Ask the girls if they would want people to do this to them.

Now take the sticky notes off Sheila: invite everyone to run up all at once and 'save' her from the labels. Rip them off her and throw them out. Part of the purpose of this group is to get to know each other better, take off labels, and make new friends.

Explain that each girl has the power to help the girls in her school get along better by learning things here in this group and then taking what they learn and making a difference in their school.

We start by being open to getting to know each other better. Each girl is different, and all are important. Some are quiet, some are loud, some like karate, some like ballet, some are smart, some are funny, some are good at math, and some like to sit and read. It would be very boring if we were all exactly the same. What if everyone talked and no one listened? What if everyone listened and no one talked? What if everyone had black hair and blue eyes? What if everyone was the same height? The world is interesting because we are all different.

The next activity will help the group have a better idea of different and similar they are.

Craft: What Makes You You (30 minutes)

Preparation: Have a variety of stickers (sports, hobbies, flowers, animals), magazine cut-outs, phrases and words, quotes, scriptures, and pictures for the girls to use to make this project. You can get these ahead of time by cutting phrases and pictures out of magazines, printing images from online, using pages from our Appendix, or purchasing from craft supply stores.

Activity: Each girl will make an individual poster so she'll be able to tell the group about herself. Show a sample about yourself you've already made to give them an idea. Spend the rest of the time making posters, and plan on finishing it next week (hold on to the posters for next week). Chat and get to know each other as you work on your crafts.

Clean Up (5 minutes)

Spend the last minutes having the girls be responsible for clean-up. This will teach the girls to take ownership of their mess and be responsible for their actions. Explain that no one can leave until everything is tidied.

Group Picture (2 minutes)

Each week, take a picture of the group before they leave. In addition, take a group picture of just those who have permission to be posted publicly.

The world
would be boring
if we were all
exactly the same.

Week 2

Objective

In this lesson, we will learn how to get to know other people, how to speak in front of a group, show respect, have good listening skills, and ask good questions. Each girl will tell about herself, using the poster she made to represent herself.

Preparation and Materials

- Make copies of the Find Someone Who Can Say game in the Appendix page 38
- Have prizes for this week's prize drawing.
- Set out the decorating supplies and posters the girls started last week.
- Have a timer ready to use
- Have "Friendship Expert" in Appendix page 41 ready for the end of the lesson.

Lesson at a Glance

Activity	What To Do	Materials
1. Find Someone Who Can Say	Mingle with group to fill game sheet	Copy in Appendix page 38, pens
2. Prize bag	Pick winners	Names in drawing bag, prizes
3. What Makes You You	Finish posters	11x14 posters, craft supplies (same as Week 1, see page 15)
4. Speaking to a group	Talk about how to speak in front of group	
5. Respectful listening	Talk about how to listen	
6. Thoughtful Questions	Learn how to ask good questions	
7. Presentations	Each girl presents their poster in two minutes	Completed posters
8. Group Picture	Take a photo	Camera/phone
9. Friendship Expert	Answer questions	Copy in Appendix page 41

Arrival, Sign in (5 minutes)

Find Someone Who Can Say . . . (7 minutes)

This game is in Appendix page 38. Make enough copies of the game for each girl to have one to write on.. Give each girl a pen. Give them enough time to mingle with each other and get their game pages signed. The goal is to complete as many squares as possible before time is up. When finished, let a few girls share something fun they discovered.

Prize Bag

Pick new names to win a prize. Throw away the winners name, so they aren't chosen again. Each person wins one time.

What Makes You You (15 minutes)

Finish work on the poster activity "What Makes You You." Try finishing in 15 minutes; the discussion and presentation are both more important than the finished product. Each girl should have two minutes to share about herself. The girls who finish ahead of time can just draw.

How to Speak in Front of a Group (5 minutes)

Demonstrate the basic rules of how to speak in front of a group, by sharing about yourself from your own poster: 1) speak loudly and clearly, 2) have eye contact, 3) let the group see your poster as you explain it, 4) as you finish, ask if anyone has questions.

Respectful Listening (5 minutes)

Discuss how to listen to people respectfully by asking the following questions.

- What are some ways you can show people you are interested in listening to them? *(Look at them, sit still, don't talk, pay attention, don't be doing other things, don't be trying to get attention on yourself, don't say t hings about yourself, think about them, think of questions you can ask them .)*
- How do you want people acting when you are the one talking?
- If someone moves, looks around, acts distracted, or talks while you are talking, what does that "say" to you?
- So when people are show us their poster, what are we are going to do? (Pay attention, watch them, look at them, look interested, do not make inappropriate comments, etc.)

Thoughtful Questions

Talk about how to ask questions in a way that makes people want to answer by using the following examples:

Which is better?

"Why do you like cats?
I can't stand them!"

"What do you like about cats?
Do you have a cat?"

"I don't like summer, it's so hot!"

"Why did you put a sticker of a sun? Does it mean you like it when it's sunny or that summer is your favorite season?"

"I've never heard your name before; that's spelled funny... that sounds weird..."

"What does your name mean? Do you know why you got named that?"

Think before you ask a question. How can you make it nicer? How can you learn something about that person? Am I putting attention on myself, or getting to know that person better? Am I asking the way I'd want to be asked?

Presentations (45 minutes)

Each person gets three minutes to show their poster and tell the group about themselves. Explain and offer two ways to do this: they can tell about themselves, or they can let the group ask questions about their poster, whichever they prefer. No need to stand in front of the group; just sit in a circle.

Have a timer out where everyone can see it. Have girls take turns and share. You may want to consider two minutes to tell about herself, and one minute for questions.

Group Picture (2 minutes)

Take a picture of the entire group.

Clean Up (3 minutes)

Spend the last minutes having the girls be responsible for help with clean-up. This will teach the girls to take ownership of their mess and be responsible for their actions. Explain that no one can leave until everything is tidied.

Extra: If there is extra time, put the girls in groups and do Friendship Expert in Appendix page 41. You might put the talkative girls together and the quiet girls together. Or do this as group discussion; read the scenarios out loud and see what girls think. Then follow up with your own thoughts.

Friends
are gifts;
treat them
like gifts.

WEEK 3

Week 3

Objective

The purpose of this lesson is to discuss different types of friends, the advantages and disadvantages of having one best friend, what makes a good friend, and how to get to know someone.

Preparation and Materials

- Items needed for today's lesson: prize bag, Friendship Pie visual, silhouette posterboard, blank circles to write on (six per girl), tape for circles, pens, and snowball papers. Blank circles can be purchased in packets. These will be written on and taped to the poster. Another option is to make your own using Appendix page 46.
- Have a copy of Icebreaker questions (Appendix page 39).
- Have Friendship Pie visual ready (Appendix page 42 is example for leader, page 43 is for the group to fill in).
- Have Silhouette ready (Appendix page 44 is example for leader, page 45 is example needed for the group project).
- Have Snowball papers ready (Appendix page 47).

Lesson at a Glance

Activity	What To Do	Materials
1. PrizeBag	Pick winners	Names in drawing bag, prizes
2. Icebreaker	Answer questions as group	Icebreaker Questions (Appendix page 39)
3. Friend Talk	Group discussion	Big notepad, 16x24 or bigger
4. Friendship Pie	Discuss where we meet friends	Friendship Pie visual (Appendix page 43)
5. Silhouette Friend	Discuss good and bad friendships	Blue posterboard with green silhouette, six circles for each girl, sharpies, tape (Appendix page 44-46)
6. Snowball	Write about current fights anonymously	Copies of Snowballs made (Appendix page 47), pens
7. Group Photo	Take a photo of all	Camera/phone

Note: You may want to begin procuring/preparing the Word Boxes for Week 5 this week. (See page 32). If purchasing boxes is not in the budget, you can also use shoe boxes or envelopes.

Prize Bag

Give out prizes to new winners.

Icebreaker (10 minutes)

Each girl gets a copy of page 39, and mills about the group asking each other questions. Encourage the girls to ask every girl a question.

Friend Talk (10 minutes)

For **Friend Talk**, use a big notepad in front of the group to write down answers to these questions as you discuss them. Be open to hearing their voices before you give thoughts of your own. This is a brainstorming event to hear their thoughts. Perhaps pick a quiet girl to write for the group.

Questions to ask:

- Is it important to girls to have a BEST friend?
- If yes, why?
- If no, why not?
- Can anyone tell me why it would be good to have lots of friends and not just one?
- Do you want your good friend to only do things with you?
- Do you get mad at her if she does stuff with other friends?
- Do you want your good friend to get mad at you when you do things with others?

After this discussion, talk about this quote: *Do you know that many, many girls in tween and teen years say they are lonely? Many wish they had more friends, or better friends. That's common. Friends are super important. Sometimes we may feel like we don't have many friends, but actually there are lots of nice people around us every day. Many girls feel this way and need new friends.*

Friendship Pie (10 minutes)

Use the Friendship Pie (Appendix page 43) to discuss and list different places in each slice where you might be able to make friends. Put a blank friendship pie up for them all to see, and ask them to share all the different places they meet people. As they share places, write one on each slice.

Possible places include school, neighborhood, cousins, brothers and sisters, church, lessons they take, sports, swimming pool, camps, books (fictional friends), and social media. This is a good time to talk about social media friends: the advantage of having met in person before they friend people on social media, discuss the pros and cons, of conversing with strangers online, etc. Ask the girls if they prefer online or in person friendships.

Once you have the pie filled, encourage the girls to pay attention to new people who may need a friend in each of those places. Encourage them that there are plenty of other places to find friends if school is not an easy place for them.

Now it's time for another fun visual to help us see how to be and choose good friends. We're going to have an imaginary friend together!

Silhouette Friend (30 minutes)

Using this object lesson, we will see what makes a good friendship and what hurts a friendship.

Prepare the blue posterboard with the green silhouette prior to class. Hold it up for the group to see and explain that this is a visual of the perfect friend. She's not real, because no one is perfect, but we can learn from her. Have the group name her together. Write her name on the poster. Today's discussion will cover positive things about friendship, represented by the green (true friendship is life-giving...green represents life). Some friendships cause problems, which make us sad, represented by the blue area ("blue" means sad).

Group discussion: what are qualities that make a good friend?

Ideas: honest, funny, stands up for me, available, nice, keeps secrets, gives good advice, caring, listens, respects, treats people well, and invites me places.

After this discussion, each girl will now narrow down three qualities that are very important to her to have in a good friend. Pass out three circles and a sharpie to each girl. Ask them to write one favorite quality on each circle.

When you're ready to discuss, have someone share a good quality and stick it on the silhouette inside the green area. Anyone who wrote the same quality can pass their word to the leader to hold. One at a time, each girl shares a quality she wrote and sticks it on the silhouette in the green area. Keep sharing qualities until all are shared, and either put on the silhouette or passed to the leader.

New group discussion: What are qualities that make a bad friend? Think about it this way: what are things that girls do that cause fights among friends?

Ideas: talks about others, lies, tells secrets, spreads rumors, bossy, leaves me out, steals my friend, laughs at me, never listens, makes me look dumb, asks me to do things that are wrong, hits, is mean to others, and only talks about herself.

After this discussion, pass out three more circles, and ask each girl to write the top three things that they don't like a friend doing, one on each circle.

Have someone share a quality and stick it on the outside of our silhouette friend, on the blue part. Anyone who wrote the same quality can pass it to the leader to set aside. One at a time, each girl shares and puts her quality on the blue part.

When all the circles are put on the blue area, hold the poster up as a visual.
- All the things on the inside are qualities that make a good friend.
- All the things on the outside are qualities that cause fights among friends.

Have the girls, without talking, think about their best couple of friends that they hang out with the most. For the most part, are they like the inside or the outside of the silhouette? (DON'T ANSWER OUT LOUD). Encourage honesty. This is a time of silent reflection.

What kind of friend are YOU? Next, have them think about where they fit. What do they do most of the time—things on the inside or on the outside? What would others say about them? (This is all silent contemplation, no out loud answers). It's important what kind of friend you are.

It is also important to realize that no one is perfect. Everyone occasionally does the items in blue. We all want to be forgiven when it's us doing the wrong. Are we quick to forgive when it's our friends doing the wrong? All friendships need forgiveness.

Here's a good friendship lesson:
Everyone makes mistakes. Everyone, good friends and bad friends, are at some point going to do SOMEthing on the outside (in the blue space, outside of the silhouette). You included. Everyone messes up. No one is perfect.
Therefore, we have to be able to forgive others for what they do. We'll all need forgiveness sometimes!
Here's the difference. Are you, or are your friends, acting in the blue area MOST of the time?

How are your friends affecting you? If you are getting in trouble, being hurt, or not becoming a better person, you should consider what kind of friends you have. Sometimes, we have to stop hanging out with friends who operate in the blue more than the green. It's good to talk to them first and let them know how you feel, because maybe they don't realize what they're doing and will change. But if they don't care or won't change, you may need to find a new friend.

If you are mostly doing things on the outside, you may want to stop and really think about your life. You won't keep friends long, or have real friends, if you operate mainly in meanness. If someone talks to you about how you are treating others, listen and learn! No one wants to be alone, but with mostly mean behavior, you might end up that way.

The good news is, everyone has a CHOICE. You can choose every day how you are going to act. You choose whether to be a good friend or a bad friend. You can choose to forgive, and you can choose who to hang out with. You can choose to talk to a friend about problems and help them learn to be a better friend too.

Snowball (8 minutes)

For **Snowball**, pass out Snowball papers (Appendix page 47) and pens to each girl. Have everyone spread out around the room and write down (anonymously) some of the real friendship problems going on for them, or problems they see among their friends. Make sure they know not to put their name on it (unless they really want to). Have them answer this question: What are some of the things that you or your friends are fighting about right now? This is for the leader's eyes only. When everyone is done writing, have them wad them up and at the count of three, have a fun snowball fight! After the snowball fight, have the girls collect them, without reading, to give to you. Emphasize that no one is allowed to read the snowballs. These are not further used at this meeting.

Note to teacher: You can read these later to find out any situations that can be talked about at a later meeting anonymously, to help the girls know how to handle their situations.

Friend Pairs (8 minutes)

If there is extra time, divide girls into pairs. Assign girls into pairs who don't know each other well.
Give them six minutes together. Each girl gets three minutes to get to know the other by asking questions. The goal is to find out new things about your partner that you didn't know already! Find something you have in common, too. If you see two girls having a hard time communicating, maybe join them for a bit.

(Halfway through, tell them to switch who is asking questions.)

Spend the last two minutes letting everyone share one thing they learned about their partner.

Clean Up (2 minutes)

Spend the last minutes having the girls be responsible for clean-up. This will teach the girls to take ownership of their mess and be responsible for their actions. Explain that no one can leave until everything is tidied.

Group Picture (2 minutes)

Take a group picture.

You don't have to like everyone, but you do need to treat others with respect. No one should be able to tell who you don't care for.

Week 4

Objective

The purpose of this lesson is to learn how girls fight, talk through how to deal with conflict, and roleplay cartoons of common issues.

Preparation and Materials

- Have copies of the Fast Friendship questions and Roleplay Cartoons ready for the group (Appendix pages 48-71).
- Have prizes ready for the prize drawing.
- A big notepad and marker are needed for today's lesson.

Lesson at a Glance

Activity	What To Do	Materials
1. Prize Bag	Pick names	Names in drawing bag, prizes
2. Fast Friendships	Get to know each other	Copies of questions (Appendix pages 48-49)
3. How Girls & Boys Fight	Answer questions	Big notepad 16x24 or bigger, marker
4. Roleplay	Act out scenarios	Cartoons (Appendix pages 50-71)
5. Group Photo	Take a photo of all the girls	Camera/Phone

Prize Bag

Pick new names to win a prize. Throw away the winners name, so they aren't chosen again. Each person wins one time.

Fast Friendship Game (30 minutes)

Today's meeting will start out with a favorite game, similar to speed dating, to help get to know each other even more. Girls sit in two lines on the floor facing each other. One side stays still and each girl on that side will hold the sheet of questions you give them (see Appendix page 48). Each girl will get to know the one in front of her by asking questions and listening to answers. When you say "Go," they all ask questions at once, until you yell "Switch." Then the side holding the paper stays still, while the other side moves one person down. Repeat until you yell "Switch." Do this until all pairs talk. Then the girls switch sides, so the ones answering will now ask questions. But give the girls a new sheet of questions (Appendix page 49) so they will learn different things about each other. (The girls love this game!)

How Girls & Boys Fight (10 minutes)

Remember last week's snowball fight, when you wrote down some real problems going on? Over the years at different schools, the problems have been very similar. I'm going to read a couple of the following samples girls have written at other schools, then let's talk about them. (These are real examples that girls have written before). Assure them that these are from other schools, not their own writings.

As you read each statement, hear thoughts from the girls, then add your own afterwards.

"I am not a part of any drama. I think it's crazy. One girl has poured chocolate milk on another girl and then drew the girl who she poured milk on with a great big head and showed everyone."

"I don't like to see my friends get bullied."

"I don't like it when I already have a partner in math and one of my friends doesn't have a partner."

"One girl was getting off a swing, so when I got to the swing, she told the teacher, and said I was stupid."

"My friend stole something from me and it hurts me."

"I think it's stupid girls are always saying 'I need a boyfriend to be happy!'"

"One time there was a new girl in gym class playing with someone else. My best friend and I were playing, then she left me and went and joined the other two. I was really jealous and so sad so I sat down on the bench."

Next, I want to ask you some questions about how girls and boys fight. (As they share, write their thoughts on the big notepad).

- What are some ways that boys fight?

  (Yell, anger, hit, fight, punch, wrestle)

- What are some ways that girls fight?

  (Leave people out, steal friends, stop talking, spread rumors. (Physical may be mentioned, but try to get them to the relational things too.))

- Which way do you think is worse? Why?

- What are probably the top two things that girls fight about?

- Do you wish girls could get along better? Why? What would change?

- Do you think it's possible for girls to get along better?

Thank you for telling us your opinions. We are now going to talk about, and role play how to handle some of these situations.

Roleplay (30 minutes)

Choose the cartoons that relate to your group from the Appendix, pages 50-71. For each scenario, describe the situation as you all look together at the illustration. Discuss each person's side, what's wrong about the situation, and brainstorm some solutions. Once you've chosen a solution, have girls take turns acting out the whole scenario, using the good solution you agreed upon.

After you have finished role playing, have the girls calm down and sit together in a group to listen to a few ending thoughts that you'll share. As they listen, hand out the **"Friendship Tips"** (see Appendix page 72) to them to look over, as you talk. They will get to take these cards home.

1. We don't own each other. Friends can have more than one friend to do things with.

2. Sometimes we have to learn how to be a more understanding friend and see things the way others may see them.

3. Occasionally, we need to protect ourselves and stand up for ourselves or others.

4. At your age, girlfriends last longer than boyfriends. Work on your friendships.

5. Everyone is trying to be the queen (the most important), but there's enough room for everyone.

6. Treat your friends like the gifts that they are.

Group Picture (3 minutes)

Take a picture of the entire group. Make sure there is one good picture to print this coming week to give the girls as a final gift. If not everyone is present each week, you may want to do a collage picture in order to include everyone.

Note: You may want to begin procuring/preparing the Word Boxes for Week 5 this week. If purchasing boxes is not in the budget, you can also use shoe boxes or envelopes.)

*Words are so powerful,
we remember them for a long time.
Sometimes we never forget them.*

WEEK 5

Objective

The purpose of this lesson is to discover how words can be atmosphere changers. You can make friends or lose friends by how you choose your words. Craft: Word Box.

Preparation and Materials

- Have final prizes ready to give away to those who haven't won yet.

- Have last week's Silhouette on hand to refer to.

- Items needed: squares of white and color paper, markers, trashcan, purchased word boxes, glue sticks, decorations (stickers, gems, paint pens), several copies of Appendix page 74-75.

- Make a Word Box ahead of time as an example to show the girls.

- Have copies of a group picture for each girl to take home with them.

- Have a copy of the "We Did It" Certificate printed for all the girls to sign.

Lesson at a Glance

Activity	What To Do	Materials
1. Prize bag	Pick names	Names in drawing bag, prizes
2. Words as Weapons	Write memories	1 small white paper each (2x3 suggested) markers.
3. Word Boxes	Write encouraging words	small blank slips of paper, pens, boxes, decorating supplies, and Encouraging Words from Appendix pages 74-75. Boxes can be purchased at a craft store or on Amazon (5x5 is suggested). (Appendix page 73)
4. Word Affirmations	Write kind things to each other	"What I Like About You" and "What I Love About Girls 101" cards (Appendix pages 76-77).
5. Group Picture		Have pictures ready to send home.

Prize Bag

Pick the last names to receive prizes.

Words as Weapons (15 minutes)

Remind girls of the traits that they listed on the silhouette from Week 3. Point out that almost all those things had to do with WORDS, so today's discussion will be about how powerful words are.

What part of our body helps us say words? (Tongue). Action: Have everyone try to talk to each other without moving their tongues. (Spend a few minutes letting them walk around trying to talk to each other like this.) Discuss how tongues are important to us! But, like a knife, they could be good, or bad.

Give the example of when you're cooking, a knife is needed to chop things up to cook it. Then a knife is needed to cut things so we can eat it. This is how knives are helpful. But how can a knife be used that is harmful? (Hear their thoughts). A knife can hurt you when used wrong. Knives can be good or bad, and tongues can be good or bad. Tongues are needed for us to talk and taste. Tongues can also be good when we're saying wonderful words to each other or singing! On the other hand, tongues can be bad when we use them to say mean words to each other. If someone says mean or hurtful things, the tongue can be like a weapon.

Pass out a piece of paper to each girl. Let them know that today is a time we are going to think about words spoken to us in the past and how they affected us.

Stop, take a breath, and close your eyes. Think back to a time in your life where someone, it could be anyone, said something really hurtful that hurt your feelings. Maybe it made you cry, made you sad, or made you scared, but it was the words that stabbed you, or made you feel small or stupid. That feeling of being stabbed is how words can be a weapon.

On the paper, write down the negative words that were said to you. Don't write your name on the paper; this is anonymous. If nothing comes to mind, be thankful! Maybe nothing has happened to you like this yet, but for many it has.

When they're finished, explain that the words that were said to them were like a weapon. Give them a chance to share how it made them FEEL (not the exact words they wrote). Be sensitive as they share.

Talk about how words stick, how words can hurt, and sometimes can't be forgotten. When a hurtful word is said, somehow it sticks in your mind. We've all probably hurt somebody with our words too at some point, just as we have been hurt by words. Ask, "Do you want your mouth to be a weapon against someone else?" No! We don't.

Next, throw away the words, as a symbol that the words no longer have power over them. Explain that as they wad the paper up and throw it in the trash can, they can choose to forgive, to move on, and to not believe the words anymore. The trash can symbolizes that they are getting rid of the words spoken against them… throwing them away. Even if the words were true, they can forgive themselves, ask forgiveness of others, and move on. (Use a small trash can you provide, so you can read the words, if desired, after the meeting is over.)

Do this all together. Ask them to wad their paper up and come throw it away when they are ready. Or give them the option to shoot a basket into the trashcan as they throw it away!

When everyone has thrown their words away, hand out one more slip of blank paper.

Word Boxes (30 minutes)

This time, as you close your eyes, think of a time when someone said very nice words to you, or gave you a compliment. As you think about how you felt, write down those nice words on the piece of paper.

We can still remember the words; words live on after they are said. They can have a positive impact or a negative one.

Have the girls share how they FELT when they heard those nice words. This time, have them share with the group what the words were! Talk about how important the words we say to ourselves are. Negative words that we say in our heads to ourselves can be harmful, even if we never say them out loud ("I can't, I'm too dumb", etc.). How do those words make you feel compared to the happy words that we just talked about? Words live on, long after they are spoken. It's more important to say positive things to ourselves and think on those things! So today we are making something to help us do that.

Girls will decorate their own Word Box (see Appendix page 73), with their name on it, to take home. The special words they just wrote down are going to be kept in the box, along with some other things. Spend some time allowing them to paint and decorate their boxes. Have paint, words, pictures, stickers, rubber cement or glue set out for them.

They'll write good, positive words to store in their box, to read when they are sad and need encouragement, or when they need to practice saying good things to themselves.

Provide blank slips for them to write their own positive words. Also provide a variety of words already cut out on slips, for them to choose from and include in their box (Appendix pages 74-75). Allow at least 30 minutes to decorate and fill boxes.

Sample list of positive thoughts:

I am wonderfully made	There is no one just like me!	I have thoughts and ideas that are important	It is good to be smart	What I think matters
I have goals and plans for my life	I have gifts and talents	God created me	I'm a leader	I'm someone's favorite person
I love to be a good friend	I am a good listener	I like to think of good ideas	I like to help others	I have an exciting purpose in life

Written Affirmations (15 minutes)

After decorating, spend the last 15 minutes writing positive notes to each other. Pass out "What I Like About You" cards to each girl.

Have each girl write one short sentence or compliment to everyone in the group—something nice about them that can be put in their box. Pass out enough cards for each girl to have one for each girl. Make sure each girl has their name on their box that is set out.

Sharing Time (10 minutes)

Have the girls write something they loved about this group on the "What I Love About Girls 101" cards. Take a few moments to have the girls share what they wrote.

We Did It

Take a moment to celebrate together with the "We Did It!" certificate. Read aloud the goal you accomplished together, then have each girl sign her name. This poster can be hung somewhere at the school, or a copy can be made for each girl to take home.

Group Picture

Hand out a group picture to each girl to keep. HUGS TO ALL!

We did it!

We completed Friendships 101

on _____ at _____.

We will do our best to be confident in who we are, take care of our friendships, and look out for those around us who may need a friend.

Appendix

Find Someone Who Can Say . . . (write their name in the box)

I'm left-handed	I've been to the dentist this month	We were born in the same month	My dad is bald	I have a sibling less than one year old	I can knit
I collect something alive for a hobby	I like to cook	I've had surgery for something	I was born in California	My mom wears glasses	We are the same height
We wear the same size shoe	This is my first year at this school	I play a musical instrument	I have six or more brothers and sisters	I have a family member who is a sports nut	I sing in the shower
We have the same favorite tv show	Have someone sign their name here	We have the same favorite book series	I have a brother or sister older than 21	I've lived here more than 5 years	I jog three times a week
I like doing math	My favorite color is blue	I have green eyes	I have a dog	I love to go camping	We like the same singer
I have red hair	My favorite color is yellow	I want to be a vet one day	I LOVE chocolate	My middle name is Anne	I play softball

Icebreaker Questions

What's your favorite food to have for dinner?

Do you know how to cook?

What do you want to be when you grow up?

What's a funny memory you can share?

Who is a great teacher you've had and why did you like them so much?

What makes a good friend?

What's a great piece of advice you've been told by someone?

What's something you like about a person in your family?

What was a hard thing you went through and what helped you through it?

What makes you laugh really hard?

What's your favorite tv show to watch?

Get to Know You Game (leaders play too!)

Write the name of the girl in the blank. You can't have anyone's name more than TWO TIMES.

_____ and I have the same favorite color.

I asked _____ where she went to kindergarten.

I told _____ a funny memory from school last year.

I introduced _____ and _____ to each other today.

_____ did 10 jumping jacks with me today.

I told _____ what I had for lunch today.

I asked _____, if they could live anywhere, where would it be?

I tried on _____'s shoes today.

I told _____ something nice about herself.

I showed _____ what position I usually wake up in.

I told _____ something funny about myself.

_____ and I both like this food: _____.

I sang the ABC's for _____.

I told _____ the name of a book I read this year.

I asked _____ what the last movie they saw was.

I asked _____ what kinds of things they do to help them fall asleep.

I told _____ what my favorite thing to do in the summer is.

I showed _____ how I can bark like a dog.

Friendship Expert

Divide into groups if you have a volunteer to be with each group. Otherwise, stay in one group so you can lead the discussion. Tell the girls they are the pretend "Friendship Expert", and you will read the questions to them. Then hear what the girls have to say for possible answers. Have a group discussion over each situation, and end by sharing your thoughts.

Dear Friendship Expert,

Some girls at my school seem so perfect at friendships. They know who is friends with whom, who is mad at whom, and what should be done about it. I want to be "in the know" like them. What should I do?

Dear Friendship Expert,

Sometimes I feel kind of dumb because I choose my own friends instead of following the group. I don't really care about what everyone else does. But other girls seem so dependent on the group. I feel so different. Am I the weird one??

Dear Friendship Expert,

My parents don't get it. They obviously see I'm growing up, but they think they have a say on who I should or shouldn't be friends with. They think they "know me so well." Help!!

Dear Friendship Expert,

I'm a little sad because my friend from last year has become friends with a new girl too. She's still nice to me and we all hang together—I even like the new girl! I just don't know if I'm still her best friend. Am I selfish? Should that bother me?

Friendship Pie Example

Friendship Pie

Silhouette Friend Example

Materials needed:

*Pre-cut silhoutte and circles before activity.
- Green and Blue poster board
- Circles (page 46)
- Glue
- Tape
- Markers

Pre-lesson Preparation

1. Trace silhouette onto green poster board, then cut.
2. Glue or tape silhouette onto blue poster board.
3. Cut circles (unless using purchased circles).

Please refer to page 23 for lesson plan.

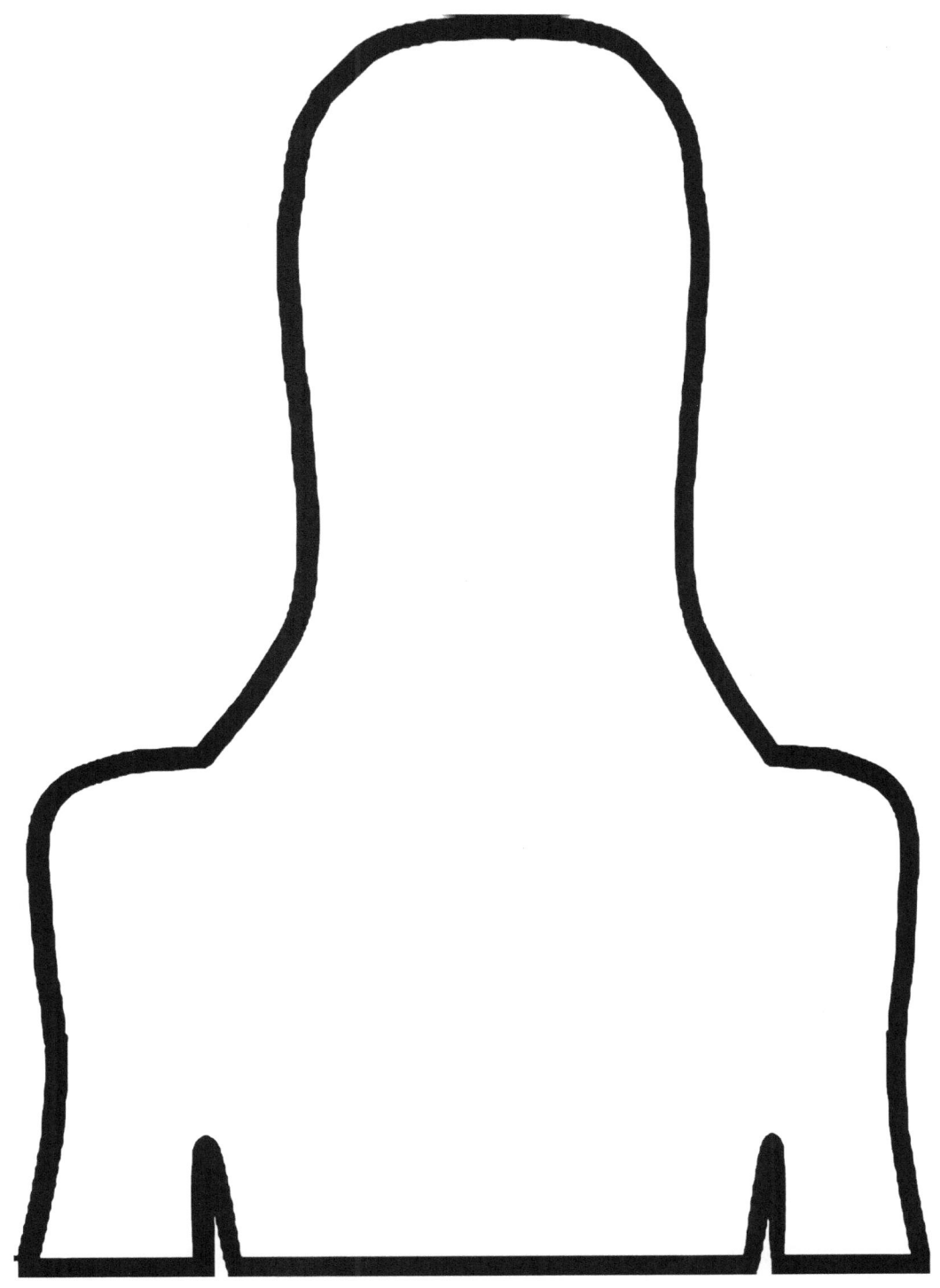

Silhouette Friend Circles

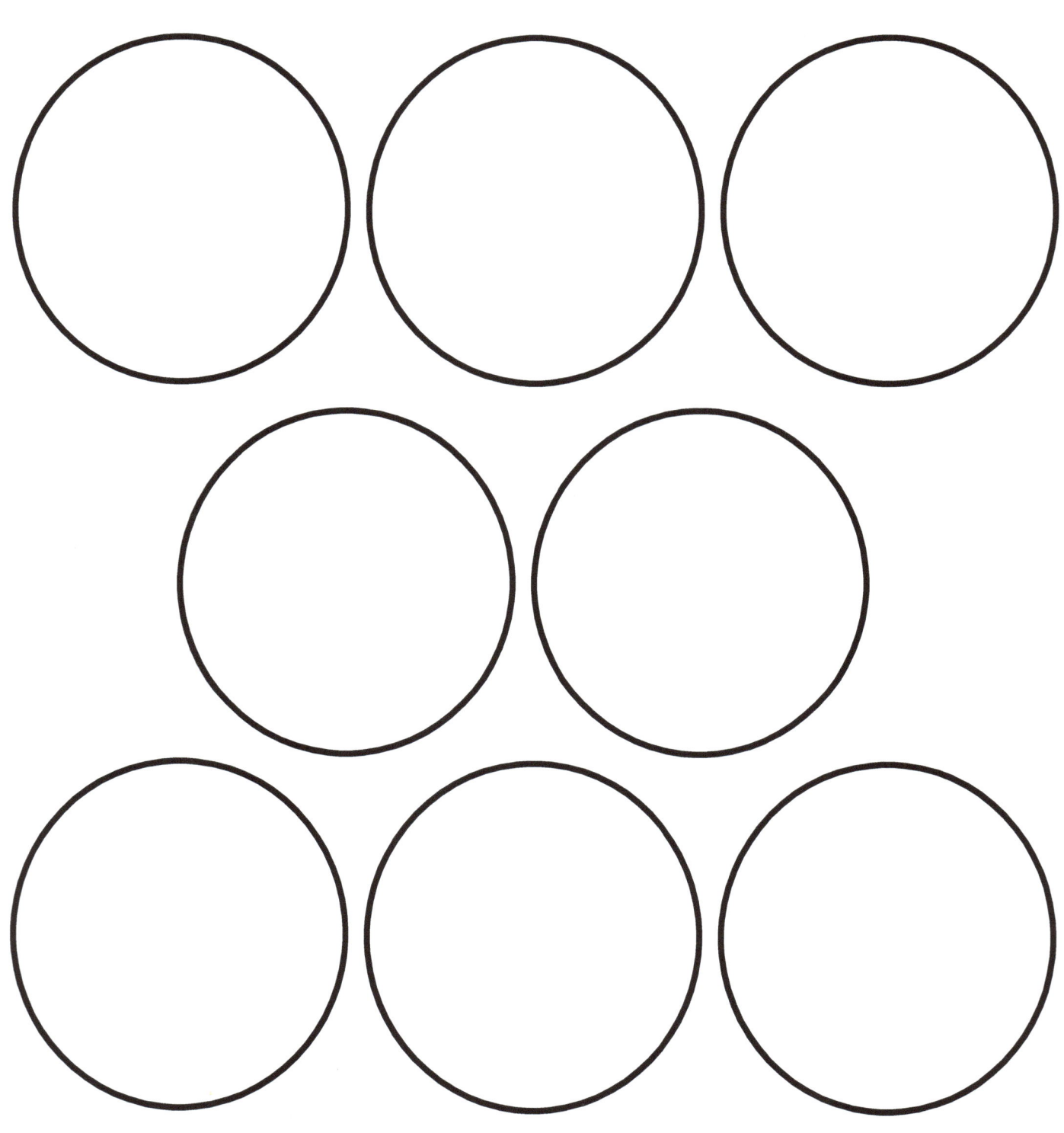

Snowball...

Snowball...

Snowball...

Snowball...

Fast Friendship — Sheet 1

What three things would you absolutely need to survive on a desert island?

Who is someone you think is incredibly beautiful on the inside?

What would your dream job be one day?

If you could have one superpower, what would it be?

Tell a funny childhood memory.

What's your favorite food?

What's the first thing you notice in a person?

What's your favorite part of the school day?

What is your most embarrassing moment you'll share?

What would you do if someone handed you $1000?

If you could interview anyone in history, who would it be, and why?

If you could trade places with someone famous for one day, who would it be?

Have you ever played a musical instrument?

What sport do you like to play?

Of the three, would you choose happiness, love, or money?

What is a song you like?

What movie have you watched lately?

What's a book you've read lately?

What's your favorite thing to do when you go home from school?

What's a job you would never want to have?

If you moved and could only take two things with you, what would they be?

Fast Friendship – Sheet 2

What's your favorite song?

What are things you look for in a good friend?

Do you have a favorite line from a movie?

What is one of your favorite family traditions, or something your family does that you enjoy?

What is a job you'd never want to do?

What's a sport you'd never want to play?

What good traits do you offer as a friend?

Who has had a great impact on your life?

What's your favorite holiday?

What's your favorite thing you've done in the summer?

What's a hobby you like to do?

What sports have you played?

Do kids in your neighborhood play outside? Do you?

What books do you like to read?

Who do you get along really well with in your family?

What's your favorite thing about Christmas?

What's a pet peeve to you? (Something that irritates you)

Can you say "toy boat, toy boat, toy boat" three times?

Can you say "she sells seashells on the seashore?"

I think they're lying to me.	
Problem	Friends lying when they're trying to keep you out of the social plans.
Possible reactions	You feel sad, they feel powerful.
Possible solutions to discuss	• Ask them if and why they're lying • Speak to adult or teacher or parent (younger girls may need this) • Forgive and move on • Make plans with a different friend (but don't team up against the other girls to get back at them) • Teach the saying, "Let it roll of you like water off a duck's back" (without immediate or lasting effects). Show the You-Tube video (11 seconds long) "Like water off a duck's back" https://www.youtube.com/watch?v=-5Gkjo10JLU. Everyone practice letting water roll off your back. Don't let things stick to you.
What would make things worse	• Begging them to let you hang out with them • Tagging along when not wanted • Being mean back to them, drawing another friend into the battle
Discussion	Any behavior that hurts someone else intentionally is wrong. Sometimes we hurt people without knowing it, and that's a different situation. What we're talking about here is when people intentionally hurt you.

A girl in your class talks so much you don't know what to do. She never lets other people talk. She says negative things about you a lot.

Problem	A girl talks nonstop and insults you a lot. She accuses you of being too sensitive when you get irritated about what she says about you.
Possible reactions	You might be irritated, annoyed, depressed, sensitive, take things personally, fight back.
Possible solutions	• Not everyone is meant to be hang-out friends. Remove yourself from her area if you can. • If you have to partner with her for a project in class, try to speak your mind too. • Be nice, but let her know you're not being overly sensitive, it would just be nice she didn't talk about all your sensitive spots. What if someone did that to her? • Talk to an adult about it if needed. She may not understand how she appears to others and may need an adult to help her understand.
What would make things worse	Fighting back, bringing others against her
Discussion	Sometimes people talk without thinking through their words. They may just be too talkative and haven't fully learned what things to say and not say. Or she may be the type of girl who wants to be in charge and dominate everyone around her in a negative way.

Problem	The girl really isn't a problem, she's just being herself. The problem here is how others are reacting to her. The girl said, "You're gross" or "You're weird," but she probably meant "You're different than me, I don't understand you." Or maybe she felt threatened by the girl's confidence. People may not understand this girl or assume she thinks too highly of herself. (Girls are sometimes threatened by real confidence).
Possible reactions	Girls may roll their eyes at her, act like she's weird, some may be drawn to her and love her entertainment and confidence.
Possible solutions	• The girls around her should not tell her she's weird or gross. They just may not understand her, or understand her confidence. They may wish they were as confident. • Let her be her, maybe befriend her! • Be polite but choose a different set of friends. But treat her with respect. • Let people be different. The world would be boring if we were all the same. And she may be famous one day! (maybe show internet stories of famous people who did not fit in during school years).
What would make things worse	Grouping with friends to speak against her
Discussion	We may not all understand each other, but it is a great characteristic to be able to appreciate different kinds of people.

I have LOTS of friends but my BFF gets MAD or JEALOUS if I talk to anyone else.
HELP!!

I love lots of friends, but my BFF gets jealous of my other friends.

Problem	A nice girl who has lots of nice friends, has a jealous best friend. The BFF gets mad whenever anyone else tries to hang out with her and her BFF.
Possible reactions	Talk about possible reactions of all three parties - the mad one, the girl in the middle, and the happy friendly friends.
Possible solutions	(You're the girl in the middle) • Tell your BFF that having other friends doesn't change her BFF status, you just want her to be a part of your bigger circle of friends too, because there are a lot of great friends out there! They are nice and want her to hang out with them too. If your BFF chooses to be a part, be extra nice in introducing her to all. • If BFF cries and stays away to keep you on her side, you may tell her you'll come over to see her later, but you're going to the mall with those girls first. And say, "I wish you would come with us" and give her a hug. • Give her a call or visit later and try to talk through things. Ask her why she is upset about it.
What would make things worse	To do as she wants and just hang with her to get her way, and not be able to have other friends too.
Discussion	No one owns each other. It's okay to want to do things with others sometimes. It's ok to let your friends have other friends too! What if you have one friend and they go out of town on a trip, or move away? Would you have any other friends?

WE DECIDED you can't play with us at recess. ALL WEEK. Until we SAY you can.

	Purposeful Exclusion
Problem	A nice girl who has lots of nice friends, has a jealous best friend. The BFF gets mad whenever anyone else tries to hang out with her and her BFF.
Possible reactions	Talk about possible reactions of all three parties - the mad one, the girl in the middle, and the happy friendly friends.
Possible solutions	(You're the girl in the middle) • Tell your BFF that having other friends doesn't change her BFF status, you just want her to be a part of your bigger circle of friends too, because there are a lot of great friends out there! They are nice and want her to hang out with them too. If your BFF chooses to be a part, be extra nice in introducing her to all. • If BFF cries and stays away to keep you on her side, you may tell her you'll come over to see her later, but you're going to the mall with those girls first. And say, "I wish you would come with us" and give her a hug. • Give her a call or visit later and try to talk through things. Ask her why she is upset about it.
What would make things worse	To do as she wants and just hang with her to get her way, and not be able to have other friends too.
Discussion	No one owns each other. It's okay to want to do things with others sometimes. It's ok to let your friends have other friends too! What if you have one friend and they go out of town on a trip, or move away? Would you have any other friends?

<div align="center">***My friend says I lied to her, but I didn't.***</div>	
Problem	My friend is mad because she thinks I lied to her, but I really didn't.
Possible reactions	You feel bad You're confused You're mad You're scared
Possible solutions	• Think about these questions. - Did you say a half truth? - Was there anything you did that she might have misunderstood? Talk about it. • Clear up any misunderstandings. Try to see it from her side. • Apologize for any misunderstandings she had or you had. Speak your side clearly. • If she is demanding you did something that you really didn't, just speak your side clearly. Apologize for any misunderstanding, but let her know you did not do what she thinks. • Let it roll off of you… move on.
What would make things worse	Stressing about it, letting the situation overtake you.
Discussion	Sometimes difficult situations like this happen to us all. Try your best to work it out.

	When you try to nicely communicate about an issue, and the other girl does not react well.
Problem	When you try to talk through a problem in a gentle, nice, mature way with a girl, she doesn't react well at all. She may assume you're being mean.
Possible reactions	Is the girl trying to discuss issues actually being mean? (no). But girls may receive it that way.
Possible solutions	• Have an adult help. Assure your friend that you're not being mean, you're trying to work things out so you can be friends with her. • Take a break, and try talking to her again later. • If she won't see your side, maybe choose someone else to hang out with. As always, be polite.
What would make things worse	If you attempt to have a discussion with someone and they don't receive it well, you may be afraid to try again in the future.
Discussion	It is good to try to talk to people. Most times it will help a friendship. It will always help you. Sometimes it will not work, but at least you tried to do the right thing.

They won't talk to me.
They must not like me.

They won't talk to me. They must not like me.

Problem	Girls whom you wish you could talk to don't talk to you.
Possible reactions	• You may be assuming they don't want to talk to you, but they may have no idea you want to talk to them • You might feel sad about yourself • You might act mean to them in response
Possible solutions	• Realize they may not even know you are around. Decide whether to reach out and introduce yourself. • If they are girls who just want to stay in their crowd, decide if it's worth it to you to be a part of that. If it is, decide how to get in. If it isn't, find other friends. • If they don't want to be friends with you, realize it's ok. Move on. Go find another friend who wants to be friends. • Are there people that YOU don't like? Realize it goes both ways. There are probably girls you don't want to hang out with. We see things more clearly when it is others doing things to us. Do we do that to others?
What would make things worse	Letting this thought stir around inside of you until it makes you too sad and you have negative thoughts about them or yourself.
Discussion	Talk about the benefit of finding out the truth about things before assuming your thoughts are the only possibility of what may be true.

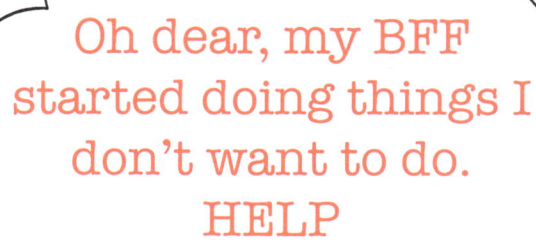

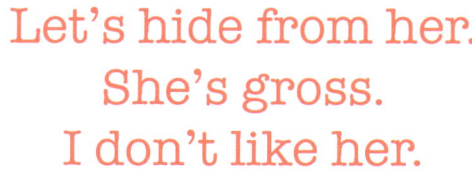

	My BFF has suddenly started doing things to other people that I don't want to be a part of.	
Problem	You and your best friend have always been fine, now this year she is starting to be mean to other girls, and you aren't comfortable being around that!
Possible reactions	• Stressed • Afraid • Sad • Confused
Possible solutions	• Talk to your friend and express your thoughts. Ask her why she is doing those things. Have an adult or older sister be part of the conversation if needed. • Tell her your concerns and what you don't want to be part of. • Tell her what you can't be around, but how much you'd miss her if you weren't around her.
What would make things worse	Joining in on her behavior.
Discussion	Are BFF's supposed to stick together even if one starts doing the wrong thing? Don't join in. Be responsible for yourself. Listen to your heart, not what others say you should do.

People who love to insult others and then say, "Just kidding!"	
Problem	A friend acts nice when she says insulting things to you, but then she always says, "Just kidding" when you're mad about her words.
Possible reactions	• You may feel annoyed, roll your eyes, not want to hang out with her anymore • You may feel confused about what she says.
Possible solutions	• Understand that's usually someone's excuse to say something rude. They do it in a way that seems nicer, but they think they can still say it if they do it that way. • Ask yourself, is she funny? Do you think she's kidding? Maybe ask her if she really is kidding or not. Tell her it comes across as mean to you or other people.
What would make things worse	To believe what she says, to fight back in the same way.
Discussion	Talk about the importance of words. It is hard to forget words that are spoken to you, and the same is true of words you speak to other people.

	I have a possessive friend who wants to do everything with me. It's annoying.
Problem	Your friend won't take no for an answer when you need to be alone, or if you do anything with anyone else. She accuses you of leaving her out and being mean to her. You like her, but she gives you no space or understanding.
Possible reactions	She might assume you are being mean. You feel obligated, but annoyed, and maybe confused as to what your obligations are.
Possible solutions	• Remind her that people are all different, and you're one of those people that needs alone time too. Not everyone does, but you really do, to feel good. • It's not a threat to her. You're not mean, just trying to feel ok. • Tell her it's normal to want to have several friends, and you'd love her to hang out with you and your other friends too. (And let her know you need alone space from them too!) • There are lots of friends to be discovered, and you want her, and for both of you to have other friends too.
What would make things worse	If you give in to her demands in place of taking care of yourself
Discussion	Talk about the different types of people you know in your life and family. There are many kinds of people. We may not always understand each other, but it's helpful to learn how to live with our differences and still be friends.

Friendship Tips

Girls 101 *We don't own each other. Friends can have more than one friend to do things with.

*Sometimes we have to learn how to be a more understanding friend and see things the way others may see them.

*Occasionally, we need to protect ourselves and stand up for ourselves or others.

*At your age, girlfriends last longer than boyfriends. Work on your friendships.

*Everyone is trying to be the queen (the most important), but there's enough room for everyone.

*Treat your friends like the gifts that they are.

Girls 101 *We don't own each other. Friends can have more than one friend to do things with.

*Sometimes we have to learn how to be a more understanding friend and see things the way others may see them.

*Occasionally, we need to protect ourselves and stand up for ourselves or others.

*At your age, girlfriends last longer than boyfriends. Work on your friendships.

*Everyone is trying to be the queen (the most important), but there's enough room for everyone.

*Treat your friends like the gifts that they are.

Girls 101 *We don't own each other. Friends can have more than one friend to do things with.

*Sometimes we have to learn how to be a more understanding friend and see things the way others may see them.

*Occasionally, we need to protect ourselves and stand up for ourselves or others.

*At your age, girlfriends last longer than boyfriends. Work on your friendships.

*Everyone is trying to be the queen (the most important), but there's enough room for everyone.

*Treat your friends like the gifts that they are.

Girls 101 *We don't own each other. Friends can have more than one friend to do things with.

*Sometimes we have to learn how to be a more understanding friend and see things the way others may see them.

*Occasionally, we need to protect ourselves and stand up for ourselves or others.

*At your age, girlfriends last longer than boyfriends. Work on your friendships.

*Everyone is trying to be the queen (the most important), but there's enough room for everyone.

*Treat your friends like the gifts that they are.

Materials needed:

Pens
Boxes
Decorating supplies
Encouraging Words (from Appendix pages 74-75).

Boxes can be purchased at a craft store or on Amazon (5x5 is suggested).

Courage doesn't always roar. Sometimes courage is the quiet voice at the end of the day saying, "I will try again tomorrow".
- Mary Anne Radmacher

As we work to create light for others, we naturally light our own way.
- Mary Anne Radmacher

Your attitude determines your direction
- Zig Ziglar

"I am a little pencil in the hand of a writing God who is sending a love letter to the world."- Mother Teresa

Today I will treat others with kindness and I will be a friend to someone in need.

The truth is important to me

I am honest and trustworthy

I have amazing potential

I will make good choices

I am
courageous

I
love
challenges

I am a
great listener

I love
to learn

I choose to move forward everyday, growing and learning as I go!

If your actions inspire others to dream more, learn more, do more, and become more, you are a leader - John Quincy Adams

God knows my heart, even if others don't

Life is beautiful and I enjoy every moment

I will live a successful life

I am a
good friend

There are people who love me

What I love about Girls 101

What I love about Girls 101

What I love about Girls 101

What I love about Girls 101

What I love about Girls 101

What I love about Girls 101

Girls 101 Foundation Presents….

A 5 Week "Friendship Series" for girls only!

Join us for a 5 week after school program for girls, as we have fun and learn about girl issues relating to FRIENDSHIP (being a good friend, choosing good friends, how to handle conflict, standing up for yourself and others).

Space is limited to 15 girls. The first 15 who return this permission slip will be part of these meetings.

We will meet on _____ from _____ - _____ on these dates: _____
(day of week)   (times)

_____

Please sign and return this form to your school by _____ to _____
(date)   (name)

Student Name:_____ Teacher: _____

Grade: _____   Age: _____   T-shirt size if applicable: _____

Parent/Guardian Name: _____ phone: _____
Address (optional):_____
Email (optional): _____

I, _____ give my daughter permission to attend the Girls 101 after school program for 5 weeks.

Please mark one:

_____ I understand pictures or videos may be used on our website or social media for promotional pictures.
_____ I do not give permission for any pictures or videos to be used publicly for any reason.

_____   _____
(signature of parent/guardian)   (relation to student)

My child will:

_____ walk home or ride a bike home after meetings.

_____ will be picked up at the front of the school at _____ (time).

Grade:
Time:
School:
Semester/Year:

Name	Week 1	Week 2	Week 3	Week 4	Week 5

www.ingramcontent.com/pod-product-compliance
Lightning Source LLC
Chambersburg PA
CBHW041617120626

46551CB00003B/476